leadership
skills

JOHN ADAIR

Chartered Institute of Personnel and Development

First published in the *Training Extras* series in 1997
Reprinted 1998
First published in the *Management Shapers* series in 1998
Reprinted 2000, 2002, 2003 (twice)

Design by Curve
Typesetting by Paperweight
Printed in Great Britain by
The Cromwell Press, Trowbridge, Wiltshire

British Library Cataloguing in Publication Data
A catalogue record for this book is available from the
British Library

ISBN
0-85292-764-9

Chartered Institute of Personnel and Development, CIPD House,
Camp Road, London SW19 4UX
Tel.: 020 8971 9000   Fax: 020 8263 3333
E-mail: cipd@cipd.co.uk   Website: www.cipd.co.uk
Incorporated by Royal Charter. Registered charity no. 1079797

leadership
skills

JOHN ADAIR

John Adair is known internationally as an author and management consultant. He has been twice listed among the 40 people who have made the greatest contributions to management thought. Over two million individuals worldwide have participated in the Action-Centred Leadership training approach that he pioneered. He was the world's first professor of leadership studies, and is at present visiting professor at the University of Exeter. He has written over 30 books, including *Effective Motivation* and *Effective Innovation*. His most recent titles are *Effective Communication*, *Effective Leadership Masterclass*, and *Adair's Management Development Exercises* (compiled by Terry Gillen and published by the CIPD). He is in addition the author of *Decision Making and Problem Solving*, which is in the CIPD's *Management Shapers* series.

Moulton College

NORTHAMPTONSHIRE

The Chartered Institute of Personnel and Development is the leading publisher of books and reports for personnel and training professionals, students, and all those concerned with the effective management and development of people at work. For full details of all our titles, please contact the Publishing Department:

tel. 020-8263 3387

fax 020-8263 3850

e-mail publish@cipd.co.uk

The catalogue of all CIPD titles can be viewed on the CIPD website:

www.cipd.co.uk/bookstore

contents

Other titles in the series:

introduction

Leadership skills have now been universally recognised as a key ingredient – some would say *the* key ingredient – in management. A *good* manager is now by definition a leader. Equally, a *good* leader will also be a manager.

But how do you become such a leader? Is it possible to develop your own abilities as a leader? Let me answer that last question with a resounding YES. As for the first question, this whole book is my answer. It is a simple practical guide for anyone who is about to take up a team leadership role in any organisation. But I hope that it will be equally useful for those already in such roles who wish to improve their basic leadership skills. If leadership matters to you, this book will give you a complete framework for becoming an effective leader.

One word of caution: nobody can teach you leadership. It is something you have to learn. You learn principally from experience. But experience or practice has to be illuminated by principles or ideas. It is when the sparks jump between the two that learning happens. So you will have to think hard, relating what I say to your experience as you read and reflecting on it. As with everything else in life, the more you put into this joint exploration of practical leadership, the more you will get out of it.

Let me add a bold claim for this short book. People often debate the differences and similarities of leadership and managership. But the majority of practical people are interested primarily in what they have to do, and not whether it should be labelled 'leadership' or 'management' or both. As a Chinese proverb says, 'What does it matter if a cat is black or white, as long as it catches mice?' This is the book for such leaders. It is the first really successful synthesis of the concepts of leadership and management. At last there is a single integrated vision, a focus that encompasses both perspectives.

what you have to be

Let's start with the most basic question of all: why is it that one person rather than another emerges, or is accepted, as a leader within a group? In other words, what is leadership? The reason for starting here is that becoming clearer about the nature and role of leadership is the biggest step that you can take towards improving your own leadership skills. In the table below, give up to five responses to that question.

What is leadership?

1	
2	
3	
4	
5	

One traditional answer to that question – which may be reflected in what you have written in the table – is that the person in mind has certain *leadership qualities*. These traits, such as courage or tenacity, tend to make such a person a leader in all circumstances. They are natural or born leaders.

There are two difficulties to this approach. First, if you compare all the lists of leadership qualities available in studies or books on the subject, you will notice considerable variations. That is not surprising, because there are over 17,000 words in the English language that describe personality and character. Secondly, the assumption that leaders are born and not made is not going to help you much. Remember that young person whose annual report stated that 'Smith is not a born leader yet'! Moreover, this assumption is not true. Naturally we do differ in terms of our potential for leadership, but potential can – and should – be developed. If you work really hard at leadership, your skills will become more habitual or unconscious. Then people will call *you* a natural leader.

Some essential qualities

You cannot leave personality and character out of leadership. There are some qualities that you have to have. Basically you should possess, exemplify, and perhaps even personify the qualities *expected or required in your working group*. I have emphasised that because it is so fundamental. Without it you will lack credibility. (Incidentally, here is one of the first differences between leaders and managers: the latter can be appointed over others in a hierarchy regardless of whether or not they have the required qualities.)

Exercise

You may like to take some paper and make a list of the five or six qualities expected in those working in your field. Check it out with colleagues. Having done this exercise myself many times – for example with production workers, sales staff, nurses, engineers, accountants – I expect that you will not find it too difficult.
Notice that *words* may vary – 'hard working' and 'industrious' for example – but the *concepts* of the traits, qualities, or abilities remain the same.

These qualities are necessary for you to be a leader, but they are not in themselves sufficient to make you be seen as one. For example, you cannot be a military leader without physical courage. But there are plenty of soldiers with physical courage who are not leaders – it is a military virtue. So what other qualities do you need?

Generic leadership traits

You will have noticed that these qualities are very much anchored in particular fields. There may well be some commonality, but certainly the degrees to which the qualities are required will vary considerably. There are, however, some more generic or transferable leadership qualities that you should recognise in yourself – you will certainly see them in other leaders. To economise on space I have put them in box form (see the table on page 6).

Qualities of leadership – across the board

Enthusiasm	Can you think of any leader that lacks enthusiasm? It is very hard to do so, isn't it?
Integrity	This is the quality that makes people trust you. And trust is essential in all human relationships – professional or private. 'Integrity' means both personal wholeness and adherence to values outside yourself – especially goodness and truth.
Toughness	Leaders are often demanding people, uncomfortable to have around because their standards are high. They are resilient and tenacious. Leaders aim to be respected, but not necessarily popular.
Fairness	Effective leaders treat individuals differently but equally. They do not have favourites. They are impartial in giving rewards and penalties for performance.
Warmth	Cold fish do not make good leaders. Leadership involves your heart as well as your mind. Loving what you are doing and caring for people are equally essential.
Humility	An odd quality, but characteristic of the very best leaders. The opposite to humility is arrogance. Who wants to work for an arrogant manager? The signs of a good leader are a willingness to listen and a lack of an overweening ego.
Confidence	Confidence is essential. People will sense whether or not you have it. So developing self-confidence is always the preliminary to becoming a leader. But don't let it become overconfidence, the first station on the track leading to arrogance.

Some readers may question the inclusion of *integrity* in this list. Are there not good leaders, such as Adolf Hitler, who totally lacked integrity? Yes, there is a useful distinction between *good leaders* and *leaders for good*. Whether or not Hitler was a good leader is a debatable matter – in some respects he was and in others he was not – but he was certainly not a leader for good. But this is all a bit academic. For leadership that does not rest on the bedrock of integrity does not last: it always collapses, and usually sooner rather than later. Why? Because that is the way of human nature.

You can see that *what you are* is an important strand in your leadership. Remember the Zulu proverb, 'I cannot hear what you are saying to me because you are shouting at me.' It is also one of the three main paths up the mountain, the three lines of answering those core questions 'What is leadership?' and 'Why does one person rather than another emerge as the leader in a group?'

Now, you can develop all these qualities. You can build your self-confidence, discover new wells of enthusiasm and grow in integrity. But it all takes time. It is better to start on one of the other two paths up the mountain. Although, having said that, I would counsel you to return to the qualities approach from time to time. Review your progress as the profile of your strengths and weaknesses (in terms of personality and character) begins to unfold and change in the positive direction. Always remain open to feedback on that score, however painful it may be (I speak from experience!).

what you have to know

Another approach to leadership plays down the idea that there are such things as generic leadership qualities. It stresses the idea that leadership depends on the *situation*. In some situations one person may emerge as the leader, in others he or she may not. Winston Churchill, for example, was a great leader in war time, but not so good in peace.

As we have seen, the truth is a little more complex than that. Some qualities are situation-related, but others – such as enthusiasm, moral courage, and stamina – are found in leaders in widely different situations.

To my mind, the main contribution of this situational approach is that it emphasises the importance of *knowledge* in working life; and knowledge is linked to *authority*. There are four forms of authority among people:

- the authority of position and rank – 'Do this because I am the boss!'

- the authority of knowledge – 'authority flows to the one who knows'

- the authority of personality – in its extreme form, charisma

● moral authority – personal authority to ask others to make sacrifices.

Nelson Mandela, for example, has dignity, integrity, and charm. Because he endured years of imprisonment he has acquired the moral authority to ask his fellow countrymen to accept difficulties and hardships on the long road to national unity and prosperity.

Why do sailors do what the captain orders when the ship is tossed to and fro in a storm? Because they sense that the captain has the knowledge of seamanship and navigation, deepened by experience of many other storms, to *know* what to do. Knowledge creates confidence in others.

For this reason your acquisition of technical and professional knowledge is actually part of your development as a leader. You are equipping yourself with one essential ingredient. To go back to Churchill for a moment, in 1940 he was the only cabinet minister with experience as a war minister in the First World War, quite apart from his own background as a professionally trained officer who, as a regimental commander, briefly served on the Western Front. Apart from his gifts of oratory and character, Churchill had a considerable amount of knowledge relevant to running a war – more so than his colleagues. And 'In the country of the blind, the one-eyed man is king.'

The same principle holds good for you. But don't imagine that having the appropriate technical or professional knowledge in itself qualifies you for leadership. Again, it is necessary but not sufficient.

Case-study: Martin Sullivan

Martin is an outstanding technician, and he was pleased when he was promoted to team leader. The technical director, Sally Henderson, in charge of production, had her doubts about Martin's abilities as a first-line manager, but promotion to a managerial role was the only way in that company of giving more money to people like Martin with long service and technical experience.

After some weeks the team's performance began to fall behind the others'. Martin knew all the answers, but he did not listen. When things began to go wrong he became more of a bully. He reduced one team member to tears in front of the others.

'But I cannot understand it,' Henderson said to the team while Martin was away for a few days recovering from stress. 'Isn't Martin a leader?' 'He certainly knows this factory backwards,' replied one of the team. 'He is a real expert. But, no, we wouldn't use the word "leader" for him. He is no leader. There is more to leadership than technical knowledge.'

All the main strands of authority – position, knowledge, and personality – are important. In order to get free and equal people to co-operate and produce great results, you need to rely upon the second and third forms of authority as well as the first. It is like a three-stranded rope. Don't entrust all your weight to one strand only.

In the first phase of your career as a leader you will probably be working in a fairly well-defined field of work, and you will have acquired the necessary professional and technical knowledge. But, within your field, situations are changing all the time. How flexible are you? Can you cope, for example, with both growth and retraction? The following check-list will help you to confirm that you are both in the right field and are also developing the flexibility to stay in charge in a variety of different situations – including some that cannot be foreseen.

Check-list: are you right for the situation?

	Yes	No
1 Do you feel that your interests, aptitudes (eg mechanical, verbal) and temperament are suited to the field you are in?	☐	☐
2 Can you identify a field where you would be more likely to emerge as a leader?	☐	☐
3 How have you developed 'the authority of knowledge'? Have you done all you can at this stage in your career to acquire the necessary professional or specialist training available?	☐	☐
4 Have you experience in more than one field or more than one industry or more than one function?	☐	☐

5 Do you take an interest in fields adjacent, and potentially relevant, to your own?	*sometimes*	☐
	never	☐
	always	☐

(continued overleaf)

		Yes	No
6 How flexible are you within your field? Are you:			
Good	You have responded to situational changes with marked flexibility of approach; you read situations well, think about them and respond with the appropriate kind of leadership.	☐	☐
Adequate	You have proved yourself in two situations, but you fear some situations; you are happiest only when the situation is normal and predictable.	☐	☐
Weak	You are highly adapted to one particular work environment and cannot stand change. You are often called rigid or inflexible.	☐	☐

3 what you need to do

A third line of thinking about leadership focuses on the group. This *group approach*, as it may be called, leads us to see leadership in terms of functions that meet group needs: what has to be *done*. In fact, if you look closely at matters involving leadership, there are always three elements or variables:

- ● the leader – qualities of personality and character

- ■ the situation – partly constant, partly varying

- ▲ the group – the followers: their needs and values.

In fact, work groups are always different, just as individuals are. After coming together they soon develop a *group personality*. So that which works in one group may not work in another. All groups and organisations are unique.

But that is only half of the truth. The other half is that work groups – like individuals – have certain needs in common. There are three areas of overlapping need which are centrally important, as illustrated overleaf.

Overlapping needs

Task need

Work groups and organisations come into being because there is a task to be done which is too big for one person. You can climb a hill or small mountain by yourself, but you cannot climb Mount Everest on your own – you need a team for that.

Why call it a need? Because pressure builds up a head of steam to accomplish the common task. People can feel very frustrated if they are prevented from doing so.

Team maintenance need

This is not so easy to perceive as the task need; as with an iceberg, much of the life of any group lies below the surface. The distinction that the task need concerns things and the second need involves people does not help much.

Again, it is best to think of groups that are threatened from without by forces aimed at their disintegration or from within by disruptive people or ideas. We can then see how they give priority to maintaining themselves against these external or internal pressures, sometimes showing great ingenuity in the process. Many of the written or unwritten rules of the group are designed to promote this unity and to maintain cohesiveness at all costs. Those who rock the boat or infringe group standards and corporate balance may expect reactions varying from friendly indulgence to downright anger. Instinctively a common feeling exists that 'United we stand, divided we fall', that good relationships, desirable in themselves, are also an essential means towards the shared end. This need to create and promote group cohesiveness I have called the *team maintenance need*. After all, everyone knows what a team is.

Individual needs

Thirdly, individuals bring into the group their own needs – not just the physical ones for food and shelter (which are largely catered for by the payment of wages these days) but also the psychological ones: recognition; a sense of doing something worthwhile; status; and the deeper needs to give to and receive from other people in a working situation. These individual needs are perhaps more profound than we sometimes realise.

They spring from the depths of our common life as human beings. They may attract us to, or repel us from, any given group. Underlying them all is the fact that people need one another not just to survive but to achieve and develop personality. This growth occurs in a whole range of social activities – friendship, marriage, neighbourhood – but inevitably work groups are extremely important because so many people spend so much of their waking time in them.

The three circles interact

Now these three areas of need overlap and influence one another. If the common task is achieved, for example, then that tends to build the team and to satisfy personal human needs in individuals. If there is a lack of cohesiveness in the team circle – a failure of team maintenance – then clearly performance in the task area will be impaired and the satisfaction of individual members reduced. Thus, as above, we can visualise the needs present in work groups as three overlapping circles.

Nowadays when I show the model on a slide or overhead I usually colour the circles red, blue, and green, for light (not pigment) refracts into these three primary colours. It is a way of suggesting that the three circles form a universal model. In whatever field you are, at whatever level of leadership – team leader, operational leader, or strategic leader – there are three things that you should always be thinking about: *task*, *team*, and *individual*. Leadership is essentially an other-centred activity – not a self-centred one.

The three-circle model is simple but not simplistic or superficial. Keeping in mind those three primary colours, we can make an analogy with what is happening when we watch a television programme: the full-colour moving pictures are made up of dots of those three primary and (in the overlapping areas) three secondary colours. It is only when you stand well back from the complex moving and talking picture of life at work that you begin to see the underlying pattern of the three circles. Of course they are not always so balanced and clear as the model suggests, but they are nonetheless there.

Towards the functional approach to leadership

What has all this got to do with leadership? Simply this: in order to achieve the common task and to maintain teamwork, certain *functions* have to be performed. And a function is what you *do*, as opposed to a quality, which is an aspect of what you *are*. For example, someone has to define the objectives, make a plan, or hold the team together if it is threatened by disruptive forces.

Now we are on firm ground. For you can learn to provide the functions of leadership which are called for by task, team, and individual needs. This is the entrance door to effective leadership. Moreover, you can – by practice, study, experience, and reflection – learn to do the functions with skill: they will become *your leadership skills*. That does not mean that you will be performing all of them all of the time.

But they will be like sharp, bright, and well-oiled tools in your tool box, ready for instant use when need calls.

Your role as leader

You can now be crystal-clear about your role as a leader. Let me explain the common but often misused word *role*. A metaphor drawn from the theatre, it points to the part assigned or assumed in the drama. In its wider social use, a role can be roughly defined as the *expectations* that people have of you. Of course, if different people have different expectations, you may experience *role conflict*. You may find, for example, that there is considerable tension at certain times in your life between the expectations of your parents, those of your life partner, and those of your children.

We do not expect people to act outside their roles in the context of work. For instance, if a policeman stopped your car simply to tell you a joke that he had heard on television the previous night, most of us would – like Queen Victoria – not be amused. We do not expect policemen to behave in that way.

This is where the three-circle model comes in: what it does for you is to define the leader's role in a visual way. People *expect* their leaders to help them to achieve the common task, to build the synergy of teamwork, and to respond to individuals and meet their needs. The overlapping circles integrate these three facets of the role.

Following the analogy of light, the leadership functions are like the spectrum of colours of the rainbow when a sunbeam is refracted through a prism (see the figure below).

In the next chapter we shall explore some practical ways in which you can perform these functions:

● at first with competence

■ after practice with skill

▲ through self-development with excellence.

Here is your challenge as a leader or leader-to-be. Competence is within your grasp, but reach out for skill, and never rest content until you have achieved excellence in leadership.

Leadership functions

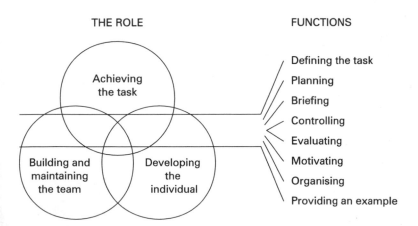

how to turn the core leadership functions into skills

In this chapter I shall consider each of the main eight leadership functions in turn, and help you to identify ways in which you can perform them better.

Remember always that – because the three areas of task, team, and individual overlap so much – any function will tend to affect all three circles. Take *planning*, for example. At first sight that appears to be solely a task function. Yet there is nothing like a bad plan to break up a team or frustrate an individual: it hits all three circles. Another general factor to bear in mind is – as I have mentioned already – leadership exists on different levels:

- ● team leadership: you are leading a team of about five to 20 people

- ■ operational leadership: you are leading a significant unit in the business or organisation, composed of a number of teams whose leaders report to you strategic leadership: you are leading a whole business or organisation, with overall accountability for the two levels of leadership below you.

Not only the three circles but the eight functions also apply at all these levels, although in different ways. In the brief discussions of each function below I shall sometimes indicate these differences, but my focus here is upon the first level – the team leadership role.

The functional approach to leadership set out here is also sometimes called *action-centred leadership*. A function is one of a group of related actions contributing to development or maintenance, just as each part of the body has its function in relation to the whole. It comes from a Latin word meaning *performance*. Sometimes it is used more widely to mean what I have called *role* – the special kind of activity proper to a professional position. Are you functional as a leader? In other words, are you capable of performing the regular functions expected of a leader?

Defining the task

'Task' is a very general word. It simply means 'something that needs to be done', usually something that you are required to do. Generally speaking, people in teams or organisations have some idea of what they are there to do, but that general sense needs to be focused onto an *objective* that is:

- clear
- concrete
- time-limited
- realistic
- challenging
- capable of evaluation.

By the last point I mean that there is a simple 'success criterion' which will enable you – and the team – to know that the objective has been achieved. If your target or goal is to reach the top of Mount Everest, for example, you will know when you attain it. In many other areas of human endeavour, of course, the success criteria are far less obvious.

Leadership is also about answering the question *why* as well as *what*. A boss may tell you *what* to do in the specific way set out above, but a leader will explain or convey to you *why* as a first and important step on the road to your free and willing co-operation – the hallmark of all true leadership. There is an overlap here with motivation, or giving others a sufficient reason or grounds for action, which we shall discuss shortly. Here I want to stay within the task circle and suggest that all leaders should be able to relate an *objective* to the wider *aims* and *purpose* of the organisation. In other words, they need to be able to think – and often to speak – in terms of a set of directions. When they do so they will be moving from the particular to the more general, from the concrete to the more abstract.

> Gaia plc are in the business of profitably making and selling drilling equipment. You could call that their *purpose*, the reason they exist. They have three *aims* in their current strategy: to improve the quality of their best-selling range of oil and gas deep-sea drills, to capture 40 per cent of the world market over the next five years (at present they have 23 per cent), and to develop a range of new products for the gem-mining market, where high profits can be made. Mike Wilson is a team leader at their Aberdeen factory. The key *objective* for his team this week is to assemble a prototype drill to be part of the company's tender for business in the new oilfields off the Falkland Islands. By the end of the week the assembled drill has to be tested against five key quality criteria and a report written on the results. It has to be in the production director's hands by 1800 hours on Friday.

If you were in Mike Wilson's shoes you could explain *why* the week's objective is important in terms of the company's aims. Equally, those aims have been identified and are being tackled *in order to* achieve the corporate purpose.

Coming the other way down Jacob's Ladder, you will be answering the question *how*. *How* are we in Gaia going to stay at the leading edge of profitably making and selling drilling equipment? Answer: by moving forwards along the

open-ended but directional paths indicated by our aims –
improving quality, increasing market share, and creating new
products.

You will notice that Gaia in this thumbnail case-study are
taking change by the hand before it takes them by the throat.
Change is perhaps the most important factor that calls for
leadership as opposed to mere management. Modern English
lead is related to Old English words meaning 'a way, journey'
and 'to travel'. It is a journey word. If you are not on a journey,
don't bother with leadership – just settle for management.

Hence leaders at all levels should stimulate and focus a sense
of direction. 'Vision' literally means to see where you are
going. Allied with some creative thinking, it can provide a
new direction for a group or an organisation. Change always
brings the necessity to think very hard about your purpose,
as well as your aims and objectives in the context of the
rapid changes in markets, technology, and economic and
social life. That kind of thinking is the prime responsibility
of strategic leaders, but if they are wise they will involve
their operational and team leaders in this process as well.
You need to understand the *why* behind the objectives you
are being asked to achieve (see the table on page 28).

Planning

Planning means building a mental bridge from where you
are now to where you want to be when you have achieved
the objective before you. The function of planning meets

Check-list: defining the task

	Yes	No
1 Are you clear about the *objectives* of your group now and for the next few years/ months, and have you agreed them with your boss?	☐	☐
2 Do you fully understand the wider *aims* and *purpose* of the organisation?	☐	☐
3 Can you relate the objectives of your group to those larger, more general intentions?	☐	☐
4 Does your present main objective have sufficient specificity? Is it defined in terms of time? Is it as concrete or tangible as you can make it?	☐	☐
5 Will the group be able to know soon for themselves if you succeed or fail? Does it have swift feedback of results?	☐	☐

the group's need to accomplish its task by answering the question *how*. But the 'how' question soon leads to 'When does this or that have to happen?' and 'Who does what?'

From the leadership perspective, the key issue is how far you should make the plan yourself or how far you should share the planning function with your team. Again there is a distinction here between leadership and management, at least in its older form. F. W. Taylor, the founder of 'scientific management', popularised the idea that things went better when there was a clear distinction between work on the one hand, such as making widgets, and the functions of planning and controlling on the other. The latter were the preserves of managers and supervisors. Do you agree?

There is a useful way of looking at the planning function as a cake that can be sliced in different proportions, as illustrated in the figure on page 30.

From the leadership angle the advantages of moving towards the right-hand side of the continuum in the figure are considerable. The more that people share decisions affecting their working life, the more they are motivated to carry them out. That is one facet of what has been called empowerment.

But, on the other hand, you will notice that when you work in the sixth position you have lost control over the outcome. The team may make a plan that, although meeting the

The planning continuum

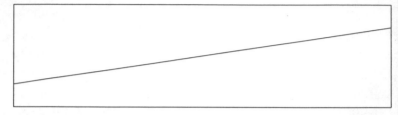

Use of authority by the leader

Area of freedom for team members

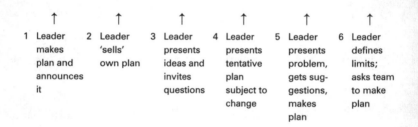

↑	↑	↑	↑	↑	↑
1 Leader makes plan and announces it	2 Leader 'sells' own plan	3 Leader presents ideas and invites questions	4 Leader presents tentative plan subject to change	5 Leader presents problem, gets suggestions, makes plan	6 Leader defines limits; asks team to make plan

requirements you have identified, is not the way you would have done it yourself. Can you live with that?

Just where you should act on the planning continuum depends on several key factors, notably the time available to plan and the competence level of the team members. There is no one right 'style'. The best leaders are consistent – you know where you stand with them and they are in many respects predictable. But when it comes to decision-making they are infinitely flexible. So a good leader, working with individuals or teams, will operate at different points on the scale during a day.

Once work has started on the plan, it may be necessary to revise or adapt the plan as circumstances or conditions dictate. Again, you must steer a middle course between the perennial need for flexibility as change unfolds and a certain persistence or tenacity in sticking to the agreed plan. Certainly, allowing too many unnecessary changes in the plan can in itself breed confusion. As the military proverb says, 'Order – counter – order – disorder.'

Briefing

Briefing is the function of communicating objectives and plans to the team. It usually involves standing or sitting in front of the team and briefing them in a face-to-face way.

Like all functions, briefing can be done with skill. For there is a right way to brief a group and a wrong way. Briefing, in fact, is part of a much larger communication skill: effective speaking. Here are some guidelines:

● *Be prepared* – rehearse and practise. Make sure that you have some professional-looking visual aids – 'A picture is worth a thousand words.'

■ *Be clear* – double check that what you are saying is not vague, ambiguous, or muddied – leave talk like that to the politicians!

▲ *Be simple* – reduce complicated matter to its simplest form without oversimplifying. Avoid technical language or jargon that your audience will not understand.

● *Be vivid* – colour your message with enthusiasm, confidence, and humour. Make it live – make it exciting and challenging and fun.

● *Be natural* – you do not need to be a great orator. Just be yourself – your best self.

Briefing is not something that you do only at the outset of a project and then forget about. Most probably, especially if the team is new or inexperienced, you will have to repeat the objective and plan as work progresses. It is always a function waiting to be performed.

Communication is the sister of leadership. Briefing points to only one skill, namely public speaking. Remember that listening is co-equal in importance. Everyone has something to contribute to the plan and its execution: ideas, suggestions, or information. You need to be a listening leader.

Briefing sessions or conferences – work meetings – allow you to do some valuable work in all three circles, making general points connected with the specific matter in hand. In the task area, for example, you can make it the occasion for taking charge by giving direction and focus. A certain amount of assertiveness is often required of leaders, and the group will accept it – even welcome it – if the situation calls for it. You can stress the team approach to the task in hand, thus building up team spirit. You can meet *individual* needs by listening to and acknowledging the help of those who help you to achieve the ends of the meeting. It can also be an

A short course on leadership

The six most important words…
'I admit I made a mistake.'

The five most important words…
'I am proud of you.'

The four most important words…
'What is your opinion?'

The three most important words…
'If you please.'

The two most important words…
'Thank you.'

The one most important word…
'We.'

And the last, least important word…
'I.'

opportunity for emphasising the significance of each individual's contribution to the success of the enterprise.

Some of the supreme examples of leadership occur when a leader takes over a demoralised group and 'turns it around'. The initial briefing meeting can be especially important in this process, for first impressions are as basic in working relationships as in love and friendship. The impression that you make on people at that first meeting will stay with them for ever. The task may have to be covered in general terms if you are new to the job – you can do little more than share your first thoughts. But you can share your vision, your spirit of resolve, and your determination to change the climate and standards of the group. That may require some tough talking, and people will wait to see if it is going to be backed up by equally firm deeds.

Controlling

Controlling is the function of ensuring that all the energy of the team, and the resources at its disposal, are turning wheels and making things happen. Sometimes teams are like inefficient old steam engines, with much of their energies escaping like hissing steam into space and doing nothing to move the iron monster forwards.

Of course humans are not machines, and *some* of their energy during the day will go into discussions or activities unrelated to the common task. Within reason this 'time-wasting' is acceptable, but it can become a problem in a team that does not have a really positive attitude to the common task.

Angela Roberts was appointed at a particularly difficult time a team leader in a factory assembling television sets. Sales were falling, complaints about quality abounded, and morale was especially low. She noticed one symptom of this poor morale on her very first day in charge. The team members in the electronics factory where she had worked before usually took a 15-minute coffee break in the mornings, but here she found that 45 minutes was nearer the norm. 'You have a controlling problem,' she told herself, and, being a good leader, by example and word she soon set a new standard.

It is the natural instinct of leaders (perhaps in contrast to managers) to rely as much as possible on self-control or self-discipline in others. The better the team and its constituent individual members, the more you can do that. The point about self-discipline is that it is our only way of both being disciplined or controlled *and* free. If control or discipline is imposed upon us – as sometimes it must be – we always lose an element of freedom. Now leadership only really exists among free and equal people, and so ultimately a large element of self-control is a necessary element of leadership. If a group or team, organisation, or community lack that, then they are also inadvertently robbing themselves of the opportunity to experience leadership as opposed to management.

'Control' comes from mediaeval Latin *contrarotulare* and originally meant 'to check accounts'. Its financial origin is a reminder that finance in different ways – profit targets and spending limits – is one important means of control. Self-managing teams (which are not the same as leaderless groups!) are those who take on board budget responsibility for planning and controlling their own work. Within limits they have discretion on how to use the resources – especially the money – that have been entrusted to them for achieving their agreed objectives.

One essential strand in the concept of management, and one that is often overlooked in leadership, is relevant here. Management implies the *efficient* use of resources as well as their *effective* use. In these days of scarce resources – people's time, money, and *material* in all its forms – the thrifty or economical use of resources is an imperative for all those who occupy organisational or community leadership roles. *Good* leaders will be managers in the sense that they husband carefully and spend to good effect the resources at their disposal. They get the maximum results with the minimum use of resources.

Evaluating

As we have already seen, a key part of defining the task is establishing the *success criteria* – by which we shall know whether we are achieving the objective or at least making progress in its general direction. Evaluating, however, is much wider than that. It is that part of practical thinking which has to do with values.

Success has to do with values, ultimately with the values of the organisation or the individual concerned. Performance has to be judged in relation to those values, which are usually implicit in the organisation's purpose. It meets the task need circle, because people need to know where they are in relation to the end result they are aiming at.

Consequently, evaluating or review is not something that you, as a leader, leave to the 'wash-up' at the end. Whenever you comment on progress – or the lack of it – or invite the team to consider their own agreed success criteria, you are performing the function of evaluating.

Because it is a major mental function, an integral part of thinking (see my *Decision Making and Problem Solving* in the *Management Shapers* series), valuing or evaluating will play a crucial role in your decision-making. When you assess the possible consequences of a decision, for example, you will be evaluating. But you also evaluate in the other two circles: the team and the individual.

Why evaluate the team, or get the team to evaluate its ways of working together? Because that is the principal way to *build* or develop the team. No team is perfect. Many are good; a few are very good; and still fewer are excellent. Here are some of the criteria or hallmarks of an excellent, high-performance team:

- *clear realistic objectives* – everyone knows what the team's objectives are and what their part in the plan is.

- *shared sense of purpose* – by which I do not mean that every member can recite the organisation's mission statement, but that you experience what engineers call a vector: direction plus energy.

▲ *best use of resources* – all resources belong to the team and are put to work according to priority.

◉ *atmosphere of openness* – excellent two-way communication between leader and members, and among members. People can speak openly, without fear of being thought critical. All that matters is to ensure that the best decisions are taken.

◉ *handles failure* – success is often to be found at the edge of failure. A high-performance team picks itself up quickly after a failure, learns the lessons, and presses forward.

◉ *rides out the storms* – the test of a high-performance team comes in the storms that overcome other, less stoutly made teams. The true evaluation of teamwork is the difficult, demanding change situation.

When it comes to teamwork, remember that success often breeds failure. Successful teams sometimes become overconfident, even arrogant, and that is when they start making 'below the water-line' mistakes, the ones that can sink your organisation. The price of excellence in teamwork is eternal vigilance.

As a leader, you should have a relationship with each member of the team – an equal but different relationship – as well as a relationship with the team as a whole. That will involve you in talking and listening to each individual. Your observations and conversations may lead you with some of them to take the role of a coach and counsellor.

If you work for an organisation you may well have to *appraise* each team member. Appraising or evaluating individual performance is actually a natural expression of leadership. If it is formalised or systematised in your organisation, you should take steps to avoid appraisal becoming a bureaucratic routine. Terry Gillen's *The Appraisal Discussion* (London, IPD, 1995) has a wealth of practical advice to offer you on that score.

Motivating

If communication is sister to leadership, then motivation is its brother. 'Motivation' comes from the Latin verb 'to move'. There is, of course, a variety of ways to move people: you can threaten them with punishments of one form or another, or induce them with financial rewards. Although motivating others in this way does fall within the compass of leadership as well as management, it is not characteristic of it.

I know that one of the things that leaders are supposed to do is to motivate people by a combination of rewards and threats – the 'carrot and stick' approach. More recent thought suggests that you and I motivate ourselves to a large extent by responding to inner needs. As a leader you must understand these needs in individuals and how they operate, so that you can work with the grain of human nature and not against it.

In this field as in the others, it is useful for you to have a sketchmap. Here A. H. Maslow's concept of a hierarchy of needs is still valuable. He suggested that individual needs are arranged in an order of prepotence: the stronger at the bottom and the weaker (but more distinctively human) at the top.

The hierarchy of needs

Physiological	Safety	Social	Esteem	Self-actualisation
Hunger	Security	Belonging	Self-respect	Growth
Thirst	Protection from danger	Acceptance	Achievement	Accomplish-ment
Sleep		Social life	Status	
		Friendship and love	Recognition	Personal development

The hierarchy of needs

● *Physiological* – our physical needs for food, shelter, warmth, sexual gratification, and other bodily functions.

■ *Safety* – the need to be free from physical danger and

the need for physical, mental, and emotional security.

▲ *Social* – the need for belonging and love, to feel part of a group or organisation, to belong or to be with someone else. Implicit in it is the need to give and receive love, to share and to be part of a family.

● *Esteem* – these needs fall into two closely related categories: self-esteem, and the esteem of others. The first includes our need to respect ourselves, to feel personal worth, adequacy, and competence. The second embraces our need for respect, praise, recognition, and status in the eyes of others.

● *Self-actualisation* – the need to achieve as much as possible, to develop one's gifts or potential to the full.

Maslow makes two interesting points. First, if one of our stronger needs is threatened, we jump down the steps of the hierarchy to defend it. You do not worry about status (see 'esteem'), for example, if you are starving (see 'physiological'). Therefore if you appear to threaten people's security by your proposed changes, then as a leader you should expect a stoutly defended response. Secondly, a satisfied need ceases to motivate. When one area of need is met, the people concerned become aware of another set of needs within them. These in turn now begin to motivate them.

There is obviously much in this theory. When the physiological and safety needs in particular have been satisfied they do not move us so strongly. How far this principle extends up the hierarchy is a matter for discussion.

Maslow's theory and other approaches based upon it are, I suggest, only a half-truth. Fifty per cent of our motivation comes from within us, as our unique pattern of individual needs unfolds inside ourselves and points us in certain directions. But the other 50 per cent comes from outside ourselves, and especially from the leadership that we encounter. I am not stating this 50/50 principle as a mathematical formula: it is just a way of saying that a very significant part of our motivation lies beyond us. Therefore as a leader you can have an immense effect upon the motivation of those around you. How do you do it? See the table opposite for some suggestions.

Inspiration is not quite the same as motivation. 'To inspire' means literally 'to breathe into' – 'inspiration' is a cousin of 'respiration'. Breath was once thought to be life – God's breath. So all inspiration was originally thought to be divine, and leadership itself – at least in its outstanding forms – was regarded as a divine gift.

What is it in a leader that inspires you? Enthusiasm, example, professional ability… there are many strands. But inspiration is found not only in the leader: the situation and the other people involved also contribute to a moment when hearts are lifted and spirits take on new life. 'The task of leadership',

Key principles for motivating others

Be motivated yourself.	If you are not fully committed and enthusiastic, how can you expect others to be?
Select people who are highly motivated.	It is not easy to motivate the unwilling. Choose those who have the seeds of high motivation within them.
Set realistic and challenging targets.	The better the team and its individual members, the more they will respond to objectives that stretch them, providing these are realistic.
Remember that progress motivates.	If you never give people feedback on how they are progressing, you will soon demotivate them.
Provide fair rewards.	Not easy. Do you reward the whole team, or each individual, or both? Either way, the perception of unfair rewards certainly works against motivation.
Give recognition.	They cost you nothing, but praise and recognition based upon performance are the oxygen of the human spirit.

John Buchan wrote, 'is not to put greatness into humanity, but to elicit, for the greatness is there already.'

Have you ever reflected on how fortunate you are to have people working in your team who have these seeds of greatness in them? Your task is to locate, release, and channel their greatness. It calls for all that is best in you.

Organising

Just as the language of leadership qualities is a bit imprecise – 'perseverance', 'tenacity', and 'stickability' mean, for instance, roughly the same thing – so the language of functions is also imprecise. Organising is the function of arranging or forming into a coherent whole. It can mean systematic planning as well, but that is a function we have already covered. It encompasses the structuring – or restructuring – that has to be done if people are to work in harness as a team, with each element performing its proper part in an effective whole. You may, for example, break a larger group down into smaller subgroups.

At first sight you may think that the organising function belongs more to the strategic and operational levels of leadership rather than to your role as a team leader. You are probably right as far as such factors as the size and structure of your group is concerned, or indeed its relations with other groups in the organisation. But here I suggest that the organising function concerns more than structuring or restructuring the architecture of organisations. If someone is described as a 'good organiser', what is meant by that phrase?

Much of the ground here has been covered already, such as being clear about the objectives, making a workable plan, and structuring the group so as to facilitate two-way communication, teamwork, and the appropriate measure of control. But there are three other aspects to be considered: systems, administration, and time management.

Systems

Organisers tend to organise things by introducing systems. A system is almost a synonym for an organisation: a set of interrelated parts making up a whole. But 'system' can refer to *processes* – orderly or structured ways of doing things – as well as social structures.

Now you cannot run anything (even a fish and chip shop) without systems: production systems, selling systems, financial systems, and so on. In large organisations there is a variety of other systems, such as an appraisal system or a quality control system.

A good leader understands the importance and value of systems. Almost by definition it is impossible to think of organisations that do not have systems or definite ways of doing things, although they are not always immediately apparent. A good leader respects and works through the systems, changing them if need be. But they are not bound by them, like prisoners shackled in chains. They know when a system is becoming counterproductive.

Moreover, every system – if you think about it – requires teamwork to make it effective. So we come back to that core metafunction of leadership: building and maintaining the team. Have you noticed, too, that systems do not learn – only people learn! Indeed, left to themselves systems are subject to one of the laws of thermodynamics: they run down and atrophy. To keep systems – the very essence of a corporate body – fit and healthy, good leadership at all levels is needed.

Administration

Administration is usually linked to management skills rather than leadership skills. You may be able to recall a leader you have met who was full of entrepreneurial spirit, enthusiasm, and drive, a motivator of others but completely useless as an organiser and administrator. Indeed, 'industrial administration' was once the name for what we now call management. The only relic of those days is the MBA – Master of Business Administration.

Administration, as we all know, involves paperwork and is primarily concerned with the day-to-day running of things. It usually includes financial administration of various kinds and levels.

Now the key thing to remember is that administration is always secondary to something else. It is a servant function. *Minister* is the Latin word for 'servant'; it comes from the familiar *minus*, 'less' (as opposed to the *magister*, 'master', derived from *magis*, 'more').

In the old days, when organisations were overstaffed, you as the leader (alias *magister*) could delegate all the day-to-day paperwork to your staff. And to some extent you still can, not least if you have the full- or part-time use of a secretary. But these days leaders – equipped with personal computers – will often have to do a great deal more administration than in the past, especially at team leader level. So being a good administrator is now a part of being a good leader.

Taking on this administrative responsibility of leadership is a way of becoming a good facilitator, for you are thereby freeing the team as a whole and its individual members to be effective, creative, and innovative. That does not mean to say that you should do all the administration – far from it. You need to delegate so that you have time to think and time to lead. But you should perform the administration that cannot be delegated (either because of its nature or because you lack anyone to delegate it to) in such a way that you are providing a good example. If *you* are late and sloppy doing the paperwork in returns, how can you expect others to be on time with their returns? Make sure that your team has a reputation for excellence in all administrative matters.

Lastly, seeing yourself in part as an administrator helps to create real teamwork in the organisation. For you will come to appreciate more and more the contributions of those in the 'backroom' of the enterprise, those who are primarily administrators. Their work may be more mundane and more behind-the-scenes, but it is vital to the success of the organisation as a whole and to your team in particular. Remember to share your success with these invisible members of your team!

Time management

Leaders need time to think, time for people – customers as well as team members – and time to grow the business. Therefore they should be skilled managers of their own time. If you cannot organise yourself, how can you organise anyone or anything else? Administering that scarce resource, your own time, is the priority for any leader.

Exercise

Keep a log of how you spend your time over a two-week period, if possible charting every half hour at work. Then go through it putting a T for Task, TM for Team Maintenance, and I for Individual Needs beside each item. You may of course put more than one of these code letters beside each item.

This exercise, properly done, will give you an idea of how much of your key resource – time – is *not* being spent in your core role as a leader.

Now ask yourself, 'What am I being paid to do?'

Time management is made up of applying some underlying principles – know your purpose, aims, and objectives, for example – and some practical policies and tips. Learning to say no, which sounds so simple, can save you a bundle of time. For a further exploration of these skills I recommend Iain Maitland's *Managing Your Time* in this series (London, IPD, 1995).

Providing an example

'Leadership *is* example,' someone once said to me. Certainly it is impossible to think of leadership without example. It may take many shapes and forms, but it has to be there.

In the context of communication, you can think of example as a prime means of communicating a message through 'body language' or non-verbal communication. Or, as the modern management proverb puts it, you have to 'walk the talk'.

Remember that you cannot avoid being an example of some kind or other, simply because the people that work with you will always observe what you are and what you do as well as what you say. 'A manager will take six months to get to know his staff,' goes a Japanese maxim, 'but they will take only six days to get to know him.' Example, in other words, is just you. But you do have some discretion as to whether it will be a *good* or *poor* example.

Exercise

Look back over your career and see if you can identify two people who have been astounding examples of *good* and *bad* leadership.

List on paper the non-verbal ways in which these examples were expressed.

What, in each case, were the effects on you?

Did others notice their example?

What effects did their example have on the group or organisation?

As a general principle we notice bad example more than good. It shouts at us more. It is always a pleasure to see good example, however, even if others seem impervious to it. It is always a sign of integrity: that wholeness that binds together what you say with what you do. A hypocrite – one who publicly preaches one thing and acts quite differently in private life – is neither setting an example nor expressing integrity. 'Do not, like some ungracious pastors do,' wrote Shakespeare, 'show us the steep and thorny way to heaven while they themselves the primrose path of dalliance tread.' There you have it.

'Pastor' means 'shepherd'. In ancient times the role of the shepherd was a model for leadership. For the shepherd had to lead his flock – or hers, because women as well as men herded sheep – on a journey to pasture (task), hold it together as a unity when wolves threatened (team maintenance), and care for each sheep (individual needs). The word *good* in the New Testament phrase 'I am the good shepherd' means in the original Greek 'skilled' or 'competent', not 'good' in the moral sense.

Now, as I have mentioned above, there is a distinction between 'good leadership' and being a 'leader for good', although it is not one I would want to press too far. You should set yourself the ideal of being both. For only 'leadership for good' works with human nature *in the long run*. Of course there will always be 'misleaders', including those who are not so in the longer term but only in as far as seizing and yielding power in the present. 'After all,' as one such put it, 'in the long run we are all dead.' Such people do not leave behind them a legacy: they die in debt to humanity.

What is a *good* example? Again, the three-circle model can help us. Look at some key questions in the table on page 52.

One very powerful form of leading by example is sharing fully in the dangers, hardships, and privations experienced by the team. What do you think of the chief executive and board of directors of an ailing, publicly quoted company who voted themselves a 60 per cent pay rise while downsizing the workforce and insisting that the remaining staff accepted only 2 per cent (less than the rate of inflation)?

Key questions for good leadership

Task	The core action of going out in front on the journey in order to show the way is a form of leading by example.
	How can you 'lead from the front' in your field?
Team	As a builder and maintainer of the team you need to maintain or change group standards – the invisible rules that hold groups together.
	How can you develop your teams' standards through the power of example?
Individual	Think of each team member as a leader in their own right. Each should be a leader in their technical or professional role, and a 'three-circle' contributor.

You can see now the importance of this function, but can it be done with skill? At first sight, no. For skill implies a conscious learning of an art. To set an example consciously in order to influence others seems to be rather manipulative. That is why I talk about *providing* an example, rather than *setting* one. For you can provide an example in an unselfconscious way, as an expression of who you are as opposed to something done for a carefully calculated effect. If example becomes a habit, you will not think about it – still less congratulate yourself on being such a good leader!

It follows that if you are going to lead effectively by example as much as by other means you will need at least modesty if not humility – that rarest of all qualities in leadership, found only in the best. The Chinese philosopher Lao-Tzu summed it up in the sixth century before the Christian era:

A leader is best
When people barely know that he exists;
Not so good when people obey and acclaim him;
Worst when they despise him.
Fail to honour people,
They fail to honour you.
But of a good leader, who talks little,
When his work is done, his aim fulfilled,
They will all say, 'We did this ourselves.'

Yes, and perhaps one day they will add about you as their leader, 'And *you* made a difference.' That is the true reward of leadership.

how to develop yourself as a leader

Much of my professional life has been spent in trying to persuade organisations of all sizes to grow their own leaders. In that work, as I once heard an American bishop say, I have had enough success to prevent me from despair and enough failure to keep me humble. But from experience and observation I have to tell you that most good leaders emerge and grow *in spite of* their organisations rather than *because of* them. Moreover, you will most probably work for five or six organisations in your career, so none of them will be quite as committed to your long-term development as you are. How then do you develop yourself as a leader?

There is no infallible system or set of systems, I am afraid. You are a unique person, with a unique path of leadership in front of you. Nobody can teach you the way: you have to find it for yourself. If it was an easy path a lot more people in leadership roles or positions would be showing the skills of leadership as outlined in these pages than is actually the case.

All I can do is share with you some practical suggestions and reflections that you may find useful. I hope that you will find them encouraging in nature, because on a journey we all need inspiration (even to write books!). As the eighteenth-century poet John Collier truly said, 'Not geniuses, but average men and women require profound stimulation, incentive towards creative effort and the nurture of great hopes.'

Be prepared

The door into leadership has 'Confidence' written upon it. You have to *want* to be a leader. It begins with a willingness to take charge. If you hate the idea of taking responsibility for the three circles, then leadership is not for you. Remain an individual contributor. 'You cannot put into yourself what God has not put there,' as a Hungarian proverb says.

Given you fulfil that basic requirement of a willingness to accept responsibility, never write yourself off as a potential leader. It is a question of getting yourself into the right field and then waiting for the right situation. But remember Louis Pasteur's famous remark that 'Fortune favours the prepared mind.' The more prepared you are, the more confident you become. Remember as a leader or leader-to-be always to *look* confident, even when you may not be feeling it inside. People will tend to take you at face value.

Be proactive

Organisations do have a vested interest in your development as a leader, because they *need* leaders. Share with them your hopes, intentions, and ambitions. You should be seeking above all opportunities to lead, be it leadership of a team or a project group. Experience is a compost heap of successes and failures. Make compost! Without it you can hardly grow as a leader.

Apart from promotion to a leadership role, organisations may well offer you – perhaps in response to a request from yourself – some leadership training. It may be either an internal or an external course. Seize these opportunities with both hands. You will be able to practise your skills and receive useful feedback. You should, of course, remain constructively critical, for not everything you hear on leadership courses or read in books is both true and practicable. But it is a key opportunity for stimulation and learning. Take any such offers.

Be reflective

Most leaders are action-centred and fairly well immersed in their work, not least because they tend to love it. You do need, of course, to be able to withdraw from time to time and take a 'helicopter view' of what is going on. These times of reflection should include your own role performance as a leader. List the things that are going well and identify some specific areas for self-improvement. This process is a natural one in any aspect of our lives – as husbands or wives, for example – but you should upgrade it into a self-learning method. It will yield you a mental list of action points aimed at improving your skills and knowledge as a leader.

Using informal or unstructured feedback is an especially important self-development tool. People are rather like mirrors or 'social reflectors': they beam back to us how we are coming across.

In this respect, however, others are imperfect receptors or mirrors, for they do not merely observe you: they also interpret what they see before giving you their feedback – solicited or unsolicited. So you do have to be cautious in using feedback. You may have to unpack the observation from the interpretation. Remember that you are only receiving others' *impressions*, not true psychological statements about the inner you. Always look for a pattern. As the proverb says:

> If one person says that you are a horse,
> Smile at them.
> If two people say that you are a horse,
> Give it some thought.
> If three people say that you are a horse,
> Go out and buy a saddle.

Feedback is a bit like the guidance mechanism in a rocket. If you received it with an open mind, looking for the truth in it, it can guide you on your path to excellence in leadership.

Never be afraid of failure. The path forwards will be strewn with the results of your failures as a leader. For the only way you can move from being a good leader – where you are now – to becoming a very good leader, even an excellent or a great one, is by aiming higher. And that is bound to generate shortfalls. But persevere. In the end they may say of you that you are a born leader!

Developing your basic confidence using the well-tested frameworks set out in this book, enlisting the help of your organisation as a partner in your leadership development, and making discriminating use of the feedback coming your way from all sources – superiors, colleagues, team members, friends, and family – are but three practical ways in which you can improve your leadership. You can doubtless think of others. It does take time, for there is no such thing as instant leadership. Therefore be patient with yourself. Aim to take a step forwards each day. Do something differently tomorrow as a result of reading this book. However small a step it is, you will be on your way. Read this book again at regular intervals: it will help you to keep moving forwards. For, as a true leader, like Wordsworth's 'Happy Warrior', you should be one who

> Looks forward, persevering to the last,
> From well to better, daily self-surpassed.

further reading

ADAIR J. *Effective Leadership*. London, Pan, 1983.

ADAIR J. *Effective Team Building*. London, Pan, 1987.

ADAIR J. *Effective Motivation*. London, Pan, 1996.

ADAIR J. *Effective Leadership Masterclass*. London, Pan, 1997.

Distance learning programme

Effective Leadership CD-ROM, available from:

Maxim Training Consultants
57 Ship Street
Brighton
Sussex BN1 1AF
(01273) 204858

Related titles in the *Management Shapers* series:

GILLEN T. *The Appraisal Discussion*. London, IPD, 1995.

HARDINGHAM A. *Working In Teams*. London, IPD, 1996.

MACKAY I. *Listening Skills*. London, IPD, 1995.

MAITLAND I. *Managing Your Time*. London, IPD, 1995.

appendix: a leadership check-list

Achieving the task

Purpose	Am I clear what my task is?
Responsibilities	Am I clear what my responsibilities are?
Objectives	Have I agreed objectives with my superior?
Working conditions	Are these right for the group?
Resources	Is there adequate authority, money, materials?
Targets	Has each member clearly defined and agreed targets?
Authority	Is the line of authority clear?
Training	Are there any gaps in the specialist skills or abilities of individuals in the group required for the task?
Priorities	Have I planned the time?
Progress	Do I check regularly and evaluate?
Supervision	In case of my absence, who covers for me?

Example	Do I set standards by my behaviour?

Building and maintaining the team

Objectives	Does the team clearly understand and accept them?
Standards	Do they know what standards of performance are expected?
Safety standards	Do they know the consequences of infringement?
Size of team	Is the size correct?
Team members	Are the right people working together?
	Is there a need for subgroups?
Team spirit	Do I look for opportunities for building teamwork into jobs?
Discipline	Are the rules seen to be unreasonable?
	Am I fair and impartial in enforcing them?
Grievances	Are grievances dealt with promptly?
	Do I take action on matters likely to disrupt the group?
Consultation	Is this genuine?

Do I encourage and welcome ideas and suggestions?

Briefing	Is this regular?
	Does it cover current plans, progress, future developments?
Represent	Am I prepared to represent and champion the feelings of the group when required?
Support	Do I visit people at their work when the team is apart?
	Do I then represent, to the individual, the whole team in my manner and encouragement?

Developing the individual

Targets	Have they been agreed and quantified?
Induction	Does he or she really know the other team members and the organisation?
Achievement	Does he or she know how his or her work contributes to the overall result?
Responsibilities	Is there a clear job description? Can I delegate more to him or her?

Authority	Does he or she have sufficient authority to achieve his or her task?
Training	Has adequate provision been made for training or retraining, both technical and as a team manager?
Recognition	Do I emphasise people's success?
	In failure, is criticism constructive?
Growth	Does he or she see a chance of development? Is there a career path?
Performance	Is this regularly reviewed?
Reward	Are work, capacity, and pay in balance?
The task	Is he or she in the right job? Has he or she the necessary resources?
The person	Do I know this person well? What makes him or her different from others?
Time/attention	Do I spend enough time with individuals in listening, developing, and counselling?
Grievances	Are these dealt with promptly?
Security	Does he or she know about pensions, redundancy, and so on?

Appraisal   Is the overall performance of each individual regularly reviewed in face-to-face discussion?

With over 105,000 members, the **Chartered Institute of Personnel and Development** is the largest organisation in Europe dealing with the management and development of people. The CIPD operates its own publishing unit, producing books and research reports for human resource practitioners, students, and general managers charged with people management responsibilities.

Currently there are over 160 titles covering the full range of personnel and development issues. The books have been commissioned from leading experts in the field and are packed with the latest information and guidance to best practice.

For free copies of the CIPD Books Catalogue, please contact the publishing department:

Tel.: 020 8263 3387
Fax: 020 8263 3850
E-mail: publish@cipd.co.uk
Web: www.cipd.co.uk/bookstore

Other titles in the *Management Shapers* series:

The Appraisal Discussion

Terry Gillen

Shows you how to make appraisal a productive and motivating experience for all levels of performer. It includes:

● assessing performance fairly and accurately

■ using feedback to improve performance

▲ handling reluctant appraisees and avoiding bias

● agreeing future objectives

● identifying development needs.

1998 96 pages   0 85292 751 7

Asking Questions

Ian MacKay
(Second Edition)

Will help you ask the 'right' questions, using the correct form to elicit a useful response. All managers need to hone their questioning skills, whether interviewing, appraising or simply exchanging ideas. This book offers guidance and helpful advice on:

- using various forms of open question – including probing, simple interrogative, opinion-seeking, hypothetical, extension and precision etc

- encouraging and drawing out speakers through supportive statements and interjections

- establishing specific facts through closed or 'direct' approaches

- avoiding counter-productive questions

- using questions in a training context.

1998 96 pages   0 85292 768 1

Assertiveness

Terry Gillen

Will help you feel naturally confident, enjoy the respect of others and easily establish productive working relationships, even with 'awkward' people. It covers:

- understanding why you behave as you do and, when that behaviour is counter-productive, knowing what to do about it

- understanding other people better

- keeping your emotions under control

- preventing others' bullying, flattering or manipulating you

- acquiring easy-to-learn techniques that you can use immediately

- developing your personal assertiveness strategy.

1998 96 pages   0 85292 769 X

Body Language at Work

Adrian Furnham

If we know how to send out the right body signals, we can open all sorts of doors for ourselves at work. If we get it wrong, those doors will be slammed in our faces. *Body Language at Work* explores how and why people communicate their attitudes, emotions and personalities in non-verbal ways.

The book examines:

- ● the nature and meaning of signals

- ■ why some personalities are easy to read and others difficult

- ▲ what our appearance, clothes and mannerisms say about us

- ● how to detect office liars and fakes.

1999 96 pages   0 85292 771 1

Conquer Your Stress

Cary L. Cooper and Stephen Palmer

In *Conquer Your Stress* two of the UK's most influential experts in stress management make clear it is frequently our misconceptions and ways of thinking that raise our stress levels. Conquering stress, they maintain, is no different from acquiring any other management skill – it just needs understanding and practice. With the help of self-assessment questionnaires and easy-to-follow activities, this perceptive book will enable you to:

- ● assess your own level and the stress-inducing ideas you hold

- ■ differentiate between negative signs of stress and positive ones of pressure

- ▲ reconsider your behaviour and health – with invaluable tips on time management, exercise, nutrition and relaxation methods

- ● avoid causing stress in others

- ● balance home and work priorities to become an effective 'life manager'.

2000 96 pages   0 85292 853 X

Constructive Feedback

Roland and Frances Bee

Practical advice on when to give feedback, how best to give it, and how to receive and use feedback yourself. It includes:

- using feedback in coaching, training, and team motivation

- distinguishing between criticism and feedback

- 10 tools of giving constructive feedback

- dealing with challenging situations and people.

1998 96 pages   0 85292 752 5

Customer Care

Frances Bee and Roland Bee

Customer Care will help you understand why caring for your customers is so important; how you can improve the service you offer; and, ultimately, how you can contribute to achieving organisational excellence. Clear, practical guidance is given on how to:

- focus on your customers and the services you provide - both internal and external

- identify your real customer needs and how best to meet them

- find out what customers actually think of your services or products

- improve communication with your customers - face to face, on the telephone or in writing

- turn customer complaints into opportunities to impress

- monitor, evaluate and continuously improve your customer care.

1999 96 pages   0 85292 776 2

Decision Making and Problem Solving

John Adair

Decision Making and Problem Solving explains the key principles for developing your thinking skills and applying them creatively and productively to every challenge. Acknowledged as an international authority on management thinking, Adair combines practical exercises with straightforward guidance on:

- ⬤ understanding the way your mind works

- ◼ adopting a structured approach to reach the best decision

- ▲ assessing risk and generating successful options for action

- ⬤ using brainstorming and lateral thinking to increase your creativity

- ⬤ creating a personal strategy to become a more effective practical thinker.

1999 96 pages   0 85292 807 6

The Disciplinary Interview

Alan Fowler

This book will ensure that you adopt the correct procedures, conduct productive interviews and manage the outcome with confidence. It includes:

- understanding the legal implications
- investigating the facts and presenting the management case
- probing the employee's case and diffusing conflict
- distinguishing between conduct and competence
- weighing up the alternatives to dismissal.

1998 96 pages   0 85292 753 3

Effective Learning

Alan Mumford

Effective Learning focuses on how we learn. It gives invaluable insights into ways in which you can develop your portfolio of skills and knowledge by managing and improving your ability to learn – positively and systematically. Practical exercises and clear guidance are given on:

- recognising the importance of 'achieved' learning

- understanding the learning process - the learning cycle and learning styles preferences

- taking best advantage of learning opportunities

- creating and implementing a personal development plan

- encouraging and managing a learning culture.

1999 96 pages   0 85292 777 0

Getting a Better Job

John Courtis

Armed with *Getting a Better Job*, by one of the UK's top recruitment experts, you can be confident that a persuasive and polished interview will secure success. This book is an indispensable companion for all job-seekers, with lively tips and practical help on:

- finding your Unique Selling-Point

- writing a compelling CV and covering letter

- researching your targets and building up useful contacts

- ensuring an interview (even if there is no vacancy)

- taking discreet advantage of the interviewer to present yourself in the best possible light

- following up to make sure you clinch the job.

1999 96 pages   0 85292 806 8

Introducing NLP

Sue Knight

The management phenomenon of the decade, neuro-linguistic programming (NLP) provides the techniques for personal growth. Use it to develop your credibility potential and value while also learning to excel at communication and interpersonal skills.

The author looks at:

● the essence of NLP and how it can work for you

■ using NLP to achieve what you really want

▲ how to build quality relationships and enhance your influence in the workplace.

1999 96 pages   0 85292 772 X

Learning for Earning

Eric Parsloe and Caroline Allen

Today, lifelong learning is a must if you want to get onwards and upwards, and if you don't take charge of your own learning, then, frankly, no one else will. *Learning for Earning* shows exactly how to set about doing this.

The authors examine:

- using interactive exercises, quizzes and games to get you thinking

- how to reflect on what you have read and relate it to your own situation

- how to use other sources of information – people, organisations – to help you

- the use and benefits of 'action promises' – the actions you intend to take after reading.

1999 96 pages   0 85292 774 6

Listening Skills

Ian MacKay
(Second Edition)

Improve your ability in this crucial management skill! Clear explanations will help you:

● recognise the inhibitors to listening

■ listen to what is really being said by analysing and evaluating the message

▲ interpret tone of voice and non-verbal signals.

1998 80 pages   0 85292 754 1

Making Meetings Work

Patrick Forsyth

Will maximise your time (both before and during meetings), clarify your aims, improve your own and others' performance and make the whole process rewarding and productive. The book is full of practical tips and advice on:

- drawing up objectives and setting realistic agendas

- deciding the who, where, and when to meet

- chairing effectively – encouraging discussion, creativity and sound decision-making

- sharpening your skills of observation, listening and questioning to get your points across

- dealing with problem participants

- handling the follow-up – turning decisions into action.

1998 96 pages   0 85292 765 7

The Manager as Coach and Mentor

Eric Parsloe
(Second Edition)

The Manager as Coach and Mentor shows how and why coaching and mentoring provide the simplest, most practical and cost-effective ways of boosting the performance of your staff. It includes straightforward guidance on:

- ● choosing coaching styles and techniques that work

- ■ understanding the roles and responsibilities of supportive mentoring

- ▲ developing the essential interpersonal skills and attributes

- ● assessing your own competence with simple exercises.

1999 96 pages   0 85292 803 3

Managing for the First Time

Cherry Mill

Managing for the first time can seem like crossing a minefield but it should be exhilarating and satisfying! Based on the insights of 'first-timers' – younger and older – from all walks of business life, and from her own recent experience, Cherry Mill provides sound advice, encouragement and a few simple priorities so you can rise to the challenge with confidence and purpose. She covers:

- navigating your first 100 days – starting with impact and the critical things to get right for long-term success

- acting the part – learning the key management tasks and skills

- overcoming tricky situations – managing former peers, older or more experienced colleagues and those who seem to oppose you

- gaining credibility with your team and the respect of senior management

- focusing on things that make a difference and prioritising time - yours and others'

- seeking a mentor and establishing networks to give you support.

2000 96 pages   0 85292 858 0

Managing Your Time

Iain Maitland

Managing Your Time will help prioritise your workload and enable you to work better, faster and, above all, more effectively. It includes down-to-earth guidance on:

- ◉ getting it right first time

- ◼ delegating successfully

- ▲ recognising time-wasting activities – and people

- ◉ tackling paperwork efficiently

- ◉ organising work practices and making the best use of travel time

- ◉ running better meetings

- ◼ handling interruptions and the unwanted telephone call.

1999 96 pages   0 85292 775 4

Motivating People

Iain Maitland

Will help you maximise individual and team skills to achieve personal, departmental and, above all, organisational goals. It provides practical insights into:

- becoming a better leader and co-ordinating winning teams

- identifying, setting and communicating achievable targets

- empowering others through simple job improvement techniques

- encouraging self-development, defining training needs and providing helpful assessment

- ensuring that pay and workplace conditions make a positive contribution to satisfaction and commitment.

1998 96 pages   0 85292 766 5

Negotiating, Persuading and Influencing

Alan Fowler

Develop the skills you need to manage your staff effectively, bargain successfully with colleagues or deal tactfully with superiors. Sound advice on:

- probing and questioning techniques

- timing your tactics and using adjournments

- conceding and compromising to find common ground

- resisting manipulative ploys

- securing and implementing agreement.

1998 96 pages   ISBN 085292 755 X

Working in Teams

Alison Hardingham

Looks at teamworking from the inside. It will give you valuable insights into how you can make a more positive and effective contribution – as team member or team leader – to ensure that your team works together and achieves together. Clear and practical guidelines are given on:

- ● understanding the nature and make-up of teams

- ■ finding out if your team is on track

- ▲ overcoming the most common teamworking problems

- ● recognising your own strengths and weaknesses as a team member

- ● giving teams the tools, techniques and organisational support they need.

1998 96 pages   0 85292 767 3